Thames Way

haiku and tanka

Diarmuid Fitzgerald

Alba Publishing

Published by Alba Publishing
P O Box 266, Uxbridge
UB9 5NX, United Kingdom
www.albapublishing.com

A catalogue record for this book is available from the British Library

ISBN: 978-1-910185-23-0

Edited, designed and typeset by Kim Richardson
All photographs: © Diarmuid Fitzgerald
Printed by Essentra

10 9 8 7 6 5 4 3 2 1

Acknowledgements
The following haiku and tanka have been published in the following
journals: 'field of daises', 'the wind', 'yellow lichen cover', 'alone
on the path', 'foam and scum', 'water', 'large buoy', 'pungent grass,
cowslip' and 'the waves' in *Blithe Spirit*; 'lazy moon', 'the stone
arch shattered', 'light', and 'sudden whoosh' in *A Hundred Gourds*;
'in the reflection' in *Presence.*

Contents

To my parents
Seamus and Mary Fitzgerald

Foreword

I first met Diarmuid in summer 2012 when he started coming along to Haiku Ireland meetings in Dublin. He was clearly a genuine haiku enthusiast and I liked the work that he was sharing. Diarmuid is an avid reader, and his time spent living in Japan gave him a clear sense of the haiku aesthetic. Since then, he has remained an active and popular member of our group.

A year later, Diarmuid asked me to mentor him in relation to a long sequence of haiku and tanka that he was working on. I agreed, and we worked on the manuscript over a dozen or so monthly sessions. That eventually became this book.

As for *Thames Way* itself, it was a privilege to work on such fine haiku and tanka with the author. Some haiku were changed and some tanka were edited into haiku. Gradually a structure and sequence emerged. It's refreshingly unusual to have such a focussed theme in a first collection.

Thames Way follows in the great tradition of Basho's *Narrow Road to the Deep North* and other epic journeys documented in literature.

I feel like I'm being taken along the bank of the Thames with Diarmuid. The poems are evocative, most of them with a visual imperative, and many featuring sounds and smells also. He is alert to the riverbank flora, and we meet others on the journey: cows, birds, insects and other humans, of course. There are too many fine haiku and tanka between these covers for me to single one out. Pick your own favourites!

Maeve O'Sullivan

LOWER

pungent grass, cowslip
bull thistle, bluebell
in the docklands –
a grasshopper beats in synch
to the drilling

sizzle of water
drying in the sloppy mud
gulls catch worms

fountain water sprays
up and down
with children laughing –
one mother reaches
for a quick kiss

no one wishes me
well on my long way
except for one old man

in the reflection
of riverside apartments;
yellow flag iris, willow herb
purple loosestrife –
clogged with rubbish

I carried this ant
across the street
by accident –
getting home must be
like going to Timbuktu

large buoy
moves left, then right
and left again –
tides keep moving
us about

white lily
trumpet in the wind –
searching
for treasure
a bee snuggles down

iron bridge –
in the space between the beams
flickering sunlight

alone on the path
a swallow flutters past –
on the other bank
many cars
hum and whoosh by

foam and scum
whirl in the canal
dancing atoms –
galaxies circle
in space

a shirtless man
with rippling abs and tanned skin
hoicks then spits

a rower
clipping the water –
with each stroke
a crow caws

old lady on a bike
red cape billowing –
persistent rain

light shifts
under the arch –
far away
golden rivulets of sand
move in the Sahara

the waves
rise…fall…rise…fall…
thoughts pass slowly

cute young man
salutes me and runs on
a snail slithers
across the path –
I pace myself between them

under the bridge
bricks of red clay
weeping tears of grime

pedestrians
come and go…
wishing I had years
to get to know each one

field of daises
softening the blank wall
of the concrete shed

thousands of nettles
tall in the field
acrid air stings my nose

taking a photo
burrs stick to my legs:
waited all this time

the stone arch shattered
in the reflection –
leaves pass over

water
over the wide weir
echoing
long after I have
moved on

children on bicycles
quickly clip along –
with blisters
I ache my way
up the path

the sky trembles
with an aeroplane
once again
water and leaves
interrupted

boat driver
tilts the wheel left
then right –
water under the keel
how slow the Thames?

MIDDLE

disused canal –
organic coffee cup
in the wild lavender

across my way
moss covered tree
busily a spider makes it home

flies congregate
on a chestnut leaf
dancing until
they swarm around me

a boat turns
in the sharp bend of river
awkwardly –
from across the bank
jazz tunes

electric lines
held straight
from pylon to pylon –
underneath
this path weaves

I come across
a couple who wait
for me to smile
as I wait for them to smile –
we pass on

gentle crinkle
of leaves underfoot
wind waves through the boughs

summer dusk –
the reflection of treetops
rippled into black blobs

lime tree
grown awkwardly
across the path
forcing walkers
around it

sudden *whoosh*
a flock of Canada geese
call in low hoots

a fat woman
throws a rock at a swan
laughs over the wild flapping

wind flicks the page
as I write
revealing
a squashed fly

white butterfly
flutters over the path
guiding me for these many steps

algae pond
covered in branches
and cans
in the sticky air
grass grows into barley

rain gone
I take off my coat
walk with a lighter tread

a crow
in midsummer heat
looking for worms
puts out a wing –
the whole span of it

a young couple
kissing by the bank –
I scrape open
the metal gate
their lips even more busy

two beech trees
lean in to make
a perfect oval –
the path runs
to the horizon

fast waves from pleasure boats
shake the reeds –
an otter darts out

in the marshes
without my map –
joyously lost

sunlight dappled across
the dusty path –
still air

torn clouds
copper ring
around the moon –
at the station
lights switch off

old rail bridge
a swan preens herself
white –
dark silted water
stagnant in the canal

crow flies off
from a wooden beam
then onto the blue, blue, blue

a bubble
goes round and round
in the puddle –
I go on and on
in rain or sunshine

alone now:
the wind rustles
my hair
hazel creaks
grass bobs

pedestrian footbridge
covered in graffiti –
a dove on the rail

lazy moon
against the darkening sky –
sprinklers shower the grass

bunch of ferns
some smooth
others serrated
in the middle
a nettle gives company

fields of barley
shift of hue
from yellow
to brown...
clouds pass

World War I monument
the town park occupied
with tulips

a green spider
swings down from a branch
the light bounces
off the thread
I've just snapped

water striders
sunning themselves
mid-river
surfing the waves
from boats

sharp screech:
the metal gate protests
at being moved

leaves of the holly tree
tickle the river
grass blades stir
I am lost
in it all

a ladybird crawls
up and down cow parsley
then up and down
my index finger
antennae wriggling

crickets sing
to each other
with fast wings –
the air humid
with desire

summer heat –
burnt corn stalks
mingled with fresh barley
dark patches extend
to the horizon

on the quivering mirror
grey clouds block
out blue sky –
a wave goes on
forever

ripples fading out
water flies dance
on the meniscus
send it rippling
again

nothing
but more river
fields and trees –
I stare but the page
is still white

concrete pillbox
built to defend England –
aeroplane noises overhead

flock of crows
eyeing me
rise up and land
in the next field
soundlessly

legs ache, toes bleed
I sweat profusely
and now
flies land on me

sunlight reflected
on stalks of barley
heads bend and grow darker

the sun goes down
reddening the river
and geese cackle –
do they fear
endless nights?

UPPER

early morning dewdrops
merging…
under the sun

cow parsley
wilted, cracking –
its flowers
smell of rot

dried-out dandelions
beside the tall grass –
a flicker of wind

long briars
choking the mucky path
tall nettles clutch
my elbows
as I weave by

a brown fly
drowns in lemonade –
I sit drinking a beer

clouds
moody in dark grey
spitting –
all I can do
is to keep walking on

a blue dragonfly
darts from stalk to stalk
dancing jerkily
with its partner

wind-blown grass
dry stone
of the ruined abbey
rough to the touch
open to the dark sky

the long grass
tickles my bare feet
touching memories

yellow lichen covers
the grey wooden gate
cracking into pieces...
sigh of the breeze
under the bridge

after heavy showers
the path
a necklace of puddles

lunch on the bank
a swan swims up –
its black beseeching eyes

a swallow flies out
suddenly drops a feather
blessing the water

crickets noise in the heat –
a crushed snail
now a lump of rubber

open field –
a fly lands on my finger
and studies me intently

startled
a mallard dashes
over the Thames –
my unsubtle feet
stamp along the path

dead tree
clean amongst the corn
clouds turn grey

smell of lavender –
the hedge covered
in early blackberries

rain hits my face
wind rips the umbrella –
through these fields
I follow the path
alone

my sneeze thunders out –
from the canopy of hazel
a crow flies away

through the soggy mud
the imprint of tracks:
wandering to where?

whisper
of the wind in the reeds –
willow branches
dip into the water
as my heart darkens

a red poppy
tattered from the wind
this summer nearly over

a nettle stoops
into the river
sends the water off
in erratic ripples

foxglove
along the bank –
faint perfume

the river –
lashed with rain
open to the drops

my legs resting
at last
journey's end
dust settles
on the train platform

Note on the collection

The haiku and tanka in this collection were written over two separate journeys up the river Thames in the summers of 2011 and 2012. I started at Tower Bridge in London and walked all the way to the source at Kemble, Gloucestershire. This sequence has been arranged to reflect the three stages of the river. The poems are arranged in rough chronological order.

Maeve O'Sullivan mentored me in the editing process. I wish to thank her for giving me invaluable critical feedback.

The cover photo is of the Thames Path near Oxford. The photograph on the title page is the Thames Path at Cliveden Reach near Cookham, Co. Berkshire. The photograph on p. 7 is of the Thames River downstream from Vauxhall Bridge, London. The photograph on p. 19 is the cliff at Cliveden Reach. The photograph on p. 37 is the path near Somerford Keynes, Co. Gloucestershire. The poem 'boat driver' alludes to Emily Dickson's poem *How Slow The Wind?* The poem 'a crow' alludes to the poem *The Black Lace Fan My Mother Gave Me* by Eavan Boland.

Diarmuid Fitzgerald, August 2015